Catholic Update
guide to
Marriage

MARY CAROL KENDZIA,
Series Editor

ST. ANTHONY MESSENGER PRESS
Cincinnati, Ohio

LIBRARY OF CONGRESS CATALOGING-IN-PUBLICATION DATA

Catholic update guide to marriage / Mary Carol Kendzia, series editor.

p. cm.

Includes bibliographical references.

ISBN 978-1-61636-062-7 (alk. paper)

1. Marriage—Religious aspects—Catholic Church. 2. Catholic Church—Doctrines. I. Kendzia, Mary Carol.

BX2250.C295 2011

234'.165--dc23

2011018768

Published by St. Anthony Messenger Press
28 W. Liberty St.
Cincinnati, OH 45202
www.AmericanCatholic.org
www.SAMPBooks.org

Printed in the United States of America.
Printed on acid-free paper.
11 12 13 14 15   5 4 3 2 1

Contents

About This Series vii

Introduction ix

Chapter One
What Is Marriage? 1

Chapter Two
Why the Sacrament of Marriage Makes a Difference 19

Chapter Three
How to Make the Sacrament of Marriage Work 37

Conclusion 49

Sources 51

Contributors 52

Suggestions for Further Reading 53

About This Series

The Catholic Update guides take the best material from our best-selling newsletters and videos to bring you up-to-the-minute resources for your faith. Topically arranged for these books, the words you'll find in these pages are the same clear, concise, authoritative information you've come to expect from the nation's most trusted faith formation series. Plus, we've designed this series with a practical focus—giving the "what," "why," and "how to" for the people in the pews.

The series takes the topics most relevant to parish life—for example, the Mass, sacraments, Scripture, the liturgical year—and draws them out in a fresh and straightforward way. The books can be read by individuals or used in a study group. They are an invaluable resource for sacramental preparation, RCIA participants, faith formation, and liturgical ministry training, and are a great tool for everyday Catholics who want to brush up on the basics.

The content for the series comes from noted authors such as Thomas Richstatter, O.F.M., Lawrence Mick, Leonard Foley, O.F.M., Carol Luebering, William H. Shannon, and others. Their theology and approach is grounded in Catholic practice and tradition, while mindful of current Church practice and teaching. We blend each author's style and approach into a voice that is clear, unified, and eminently readable.

Enrich your knowledge and practice of the Catholic faith with the helpful topics in the Catholic Update Guide series.

Mary Carol Kendzia
Series Editor

Introduction

For Christians marriage is a sacrament. Like baptism and Holy Eucharist, marriage between Christians is a sign of God's presence and power in the world. St. Paul said that the loyalty and love in a Christian marriage are to be a reflection of the union between Christ and the Church. Anyone who seeks assurance that God is always faithful, loving and forgiving should find it lived out in a Christian marriage. Because it is a sign of God's love, marriage is for a lifetime. When Christians marry they are making a commitment not only to their marriage partners but also to Christ. And Christ in turn makes a commitment to them.

This description of marriage may be intimidating to some or pious gibberish to others. In the pages of this book we will explore what the Church means in calling marriage a sacrament.

We will see that in Christ marriage is more than an agreement or contract, more than two people living out a commitment, even more than "living happily ever after."

Using the insights and experiences of several faith-filled people, we will pursue the what, why, and how of a sacramental marriage. By the time you get to the end of this book you should be able to write the conclusion of this sentence: "A sacramental marriage is…". And your conclusion will give you a sense of direction for living a marriage characterized by love, forgiveness, fidelity, and room for Christ.

CHAPTER ONE

What Is Marriage?

The Catholic Church thinks of marriage as "the intimate partnership of life and love...established by the Creator and qualified by His laws, and...rooted in the conjugal covenant of irrevocable personal consent" (*Gaudium et Spes*, 48). That rather weighty conclusion is the result of centuries of reflection upon and experience of marriage and married life. In this chapter Fr. Thomas Richstatter, O.F.M., and Carol Luebering explore both the sacramentality of marriage and the responses of love required in the various stages of married life. Their analyses help us to see marriage as an intimate participation in God's plan and as a sign of God's faithful love for the world.

Sacramentality of Marriage

What is marriage? It may seem that a priest like me is not the one to answer that question. I am not married; I have never been married and I don't intend to get married—which doesn't exactly qualify me to talk about marriage. Yet marriage is certainly a worthy topic for discussion. It is something that needs to be more clearly understood and more deeply appreciated. But this chapter is not about marriage, it is about the sacrament of marriage.

Although I am not married myself, I have experienced the sacrament of Marriage. I have witnessed the marriages of friends and parishioners. I have participated in the wedding ceremony many times. In fact, the sacrament of Marriage was the first sacrament that I experienced. Even before my infant baptism I was born into a Christian marriage. What I am going to say about the sacrament is drawn from my experience of my parents and the many married couples with whom I have discussed the meaning of the sacrament—couples from the Christian Family Movement and Marriage Encounter—and the hundreds of couples whom I have helped prepare for marriage. These couples have often told me of the meaning which they find in this sacrament. As I have meditated on the passages of Scripture which couples have selected for their wedding ceremonies and asked me to preach about, I have come to the following conclusion: Marriage involves embarking on a new life project.

A New Life Project

We each have something that we want to do with our lives: something we want to become. It may take us a while to find out what that "something" is, but eventually a life project forms, either consciously or unconsciously. And it seems to me that as people pursue this goal, whatever it may be—to be a skilled surgeon, to be the best kindergarten teacher that ever lived, to own a farm, or whatever else they may see their life to be about—they sometimes encounter another human being to whom they are so attracted that the love of this other person supersedes all other life goals and ambitions. They undertake a new life project.

Little by little they decide that first on their agenda is now going to be the life, the happiness, the holiness of this other person. The good of this other takes precedence even over the desires and dreams they have for themselves. And when that other makes the same decision, together the two embark on a whole new adventure. It seems to me that this is the basic meaning of the sacrament of marriage.

The sacrament reveals the religious dimension of marriage. Besides the human, social, and legal dimensions of marriage—the public sign that one gives oneself totally to this other person— sacramental marriage is also a public statement about God. The celebration of each of the sacraments reveals something of this ultimate reality: who God is and who God is for us.

In the Scriptures the relationship between God and God's people is often described in terms of a marriage. The early Christians, reflecting on Christ's love for us, also used this image. Christ and the Church embrace in mutual love and self-giving, even as do husband and wife: "'For this reason a man will leave his father and mother and be joined to his wife, and the two will become one flesh.' This is a great mystery, and I am applying it to Christ and the church" (Ephesians 5:31–32).

The Catholic Wedding

Marriage was around a long time before Jesus. His parents were married, and at least some of the apostles were married. For example, in all three of the Synoptic Gospels we hear of Peter's mother-in-law (Matthew 8:14; Mark 1:30; Luke 4:38). In the early Church, Christians got married like anyone else in the cultures where they lived. Gradually, Christians began to see that the loving union of husband and wife spoke to them not only about family values but also about God's values.

There was a time when the bride's father (owner) brought (dragged) the bride before the magistrate and exchanged her for a sum of money (the bride price) paid by the groom.

When the father no longer "sold" the girl, he "gave her away." Many couples today find this symbol works against the meaning of their wedding ceremony. They want their ceremony to speak of families, couples, mutuality. They arrange the procession so that the attendants enter together as couples. The groom enters with his father and mother and the bride with hers. At the front of the church they symbolically take leave of their parents and come together and speak a word of welcome to the assembly and invite them to pray that God will bless what they are about to do.

The couple then come before the Christian assembly and vow that their love will be a sign and sacrament of God's love for us. And the community prays for them and with them that we may receive this sign and that we may, by our faithful love, support their vows.

Whose Wedding Is It?

It is the bride and groom who perform the marriage. The priest, the attendants and the congregation *witness* what the bride and groom do. The bride and groom come forward and, before the congregation, the priest and the official witnesses, pronounce their vows. Today most couples choose to say the entire text of their vows to one another rather than merely saying, "I do." They exchange rings as a sign of their love and fidelity and seal their vows with a kiss.

Normally when two Catholics exchange these vows, they do so in the context of Eucharist. All that marriage says about God's love and desire to be one with us, Eucharist says in an even more all-embracing way. Bread and wine are brought to the altar, the priest proclaims the great prayer of praise and thanksgiving (the

Eucharistic Prayer) and we approach the altar to receive Holy Communion—the living sign of God's desire to be one with us. And then a final blessing sends the bride and groom and the whole Christian community forth to bear witness to God's love for the world.

Marriage is a covenant "by which a man and woman establish between themselves a partnership for the whole of life" (*Catechism of the Catholic Church*, #1601). Usually we think of this covenant in a rather personal and individual context: It exists for the good of the spouses and the good of their children. We sometimes think of the wedding ceremony which establishes this covenant as belonging to the bride and groom, as if it were their wedding alone.

The Second Vatican Council reminds us that the marriage covenant exists not only for the good of the partners and their children, but also for the good of the Church and the good of society at large (see *Church in the Modern World*, 48).

In the years following the Second Vatican Council one of the important changes that has taken place in our understanding of the sacraments is that we are coming to realize more and more that sacraments are "not private functions, but are celebrations belonging to the Church....Liturgical services involve the whole Body of the Church; they manifest it and have effects upon it" (*Constitution on the Liturgy*, 26).

Clearly, a wedding has an intimate and personal relation to the bride and groom. In many important ways, it is their wedding. But a Christian wedding is also an ecclesial event. The *Catechism of the Catholic Church* explains:

> In the Latin Rite the celebration of marriage between two Catholic faithful normally takes place during Holy Mass, because of the connection of all the sacraments with the Paschal mystery of Christ. In the Eucharist the memorial of the New Covenant is realized, the New Covenant in which Christ has united himself forever to the Church, his beloved bride for whom he gave himself up. It is therefore fitting that the spouses should seal their consent to give themselves to each other through the offering of their own lives by uniting it to the offering of Christ for his Church made present in the Eucharistic sacrifice, and by receiving the Eucharist so that, communicating in the same Body and the same Blood of Christ, they may form but 'one body' in Christ. (*CCC,* #1621)

What Makes a Marriage?

Sometimes you can learn a lot about something by looking at its opposite. We can learn about the marriage sacrament by considering what leads the Church, in the case of annulments, to see that two people never were truly married.

"An annulment is just a Catholic way of getting a divorce." I have heard this said by many people in many different circumstances (and there are times when I feel that there is an element of truth in this statement). Yet I remain convinced that an annulment is a very different thing from a divorce. Divorce is the legal dissolution of a marriage. An annulment is the legal declaration that a valid sacramental marriage never existed.

In order for a Christian marriage to take place the man and woman must be capable of entering into such a sacrament. The individuals must have the capacity to give such a gift. This capacity develops gradually. When we were children our parents taught us little by little to be generous—first with things, then with ourselves. We were taught to share toys, playthings, bicycles, and birthday cake. Little by little, we learned to share our time and ourselves.

This gradual learning to give of ourselves is the necessary preparation for marriage. A person who has not journeyed sufficiently on the road to maturity and generosity is not capable of a true marriage, even though he or she may be quite capable of sharing an apartment or conceiving a child.

There are many reasons why two particular people cannot join their lives in the marriage project. It is not always a culpable lack of generosity. Sometimes it becomes apparent only years after the wedding ceremony that there was no marriage there in the first place. To declare publicly that the marriage never existed is what Catholics call an *annulment*.

The Church does not say that a sacramental marriage comes to an end because we consider the love of the husband and wife to be a sign of God's unending love for us.

God's love for us can never end in divorce. God is faithful even if we are not. The Church desires that even if one of the partners of a marriage is faithless to the marriage bond, the other, by remaining faithful, gives a powerful witness to the community of the way God loves us.

Our Marriage Covenant With God

In each of the sacraments a window opens and we can glimpse the mystery of God and God's plan for the salvation of the world. In Christian marriage we see that God was not content to be alone, but embarked on a whole new life project. Out of love God created us and all that is. God is faithful no matter what. Whether we are faithful or faithless, God is faithful; whether we wander away in sin or remain in the embrace of love, God is always there and is ever ready to embrace us.

This sacramental sign, which the husband and wife give to each other, they also give to the entire community of witnesses. I, too, have made commitments to God and God has made commitments to me. There are times when I wonder if God will be faithful. I have never seen God, but I can see the fidelity of Christian husbands and wives. Their love for each other is a sacramental sign and witness of God's love for me. I believe that our human lives are interconnected, like a fabric, woven together by many commitments. The fidelity of their commitment strengthens my own commitments.

This indeed is a great mystery. It is something that touches me deeply each time I experience a Christian wedding and each time I experience the sacramental love of husband and wife.

Love in the Stages of Married Life

In her reflections on married life, writer Carol Luebering recalled that from her earliest years she never had any doubt that marriage was to be her vocation:

Marriage is a vocation, so I learned in Catholic elementary school. And I never had any doubt that it was my vocation. I was surprised by the good grade I got on the vocation essay we were assigned to write in the eighth grade, for I wrote about marriage and motherhood. Those who aspired to "higher things" wrote about the priesthood and religious life—at least that was a common way of thinking.

From ancient Christian times, marriage was generally seen as a lesser choice. St. Paul considered it a concession to human sexual urges that was better than burning with passion (see 1 Corinthians 7:6–9). The Church spoke of married lovemaking as having a primary end (procreation) and a secondary end (mutual assistance of the spouses and the remedy of concupiscence). Vatican II reiterated that marriage and conjugal love are ordained for the procreation of children, and then added that marriage is not solely for procreation, but also for the mutual love of the spouses (*Gaudium et Spes*, 50; Canon #1055).

On our wedding day, the rite spoke of marriage as a sign a couple makes to the rest of the community of Christ's love for the Church. Now I know that learning to become that sign is a life-long calling, a constant divine whisper in the ear. It is more than a promise made in one sacramental moment; it is an ongoing process of discovering God and learning what God is like from the experience of married life from honeymoon to old age. This chapter will explore how those gifts grace the seasons of a married couple's lives and enrich the life of those around them.

Learning God's Other Name

There is, someone once said, no surprise as magical as the surprise of being loved: It is God's finger on one's shoulder. Feeling that touch sets the world a-quiver with wonder and teaches a couple that God's other name is Love—that, as Scripture has it, God is love (see 1 John 4:7–16). I suspect it is that sense that love is something larger than two people, not just the desire for a pretty church wedding, that sends couples to the rectory door when they decide to marry. The natural response to an encounter with God is prayer—the prayers of the wedding ritual as well as the prayers each breathes alone and the prayer they share.

The prayers of the rite stress that husband and wife are themselves the ministers of the sacrament. They become living signs of God's love; their union is a sign of Christ's love for the Church. They share their love first with each other and then with the world around them. The spirituality of marriage reflects the sense that God is part of it through good times and bad. The presence of God is what makes Christian marriage truly sacramental.

Rejoicing With the Creator

Ever since Adam gasped in wonder at the creature who was like him and yet so deliciously different, the honeymoon phase has been a romp in the garden, a discovery of creation's goodness. As they explore the many moods of lovemaking—tender, passionate, playful—and the various ways they can give pleasure to each other, newlyweds sing with the psalmist: "I praise you, for I am fearfully and wonderfully made" (Psalm 139:14).

The delights of physical intimacy are not the only surprises. I had forgotten how little newlyweds know about each other, no matter how long their courtship, until we had a recent bride and groom as weekend guests. "You do?" she exclaimed in response to something he said. "I didn't know that!"

The surprises aren't always pleasing. Men and women are different in more ways than the obvious, whether by nature or by training. And any given couple differ in the family-shaped expectations they bring to a marriage, in personality, in habits, in the rhythms of daily life. The first task is to get to know (not necessarily to understand) how the other ticks.

A bit of mystery perhaps keeps a marriage interesting. But it also makes me think that God has a truly infinite sense of humor. Why else would God think true unity possible between two such disparate creatures? Perhaps the big bang that set the universe spinning was a cosmic laugh. Certainly a sense of humor is the salt that makes the effort of learning to live together palatable. This is the stage when couples begin to learn the art of compromise, to learn to appreciate the other's uniqueness in a union that necessarily differs from the marriages of other unique individuals—skills that enrich community life as well.

Beginning a marriage means learning to accommodate the differences. Small differences loom large for newlyweds, from how to hang toilet paper or Christmas tree icicles, how much conversation is possible before breakfast to how much mess is tolerable. Then there are bigger ones to resolve: defining roles, dealing with in-laws, and dividing household chores.

Humor may smooth the journey. But it takes hard work, too. There comes (for the first time, not the last!) a point when the glow wears off, when faults stand out, differences seem insurmountable, and loving a spouse feels more like trying to love an enemy. Jesus said it is possible to love even an enemy. Indeed, he demands it of his followers. So it's back to "for better or worse," to carefully recalling what first attracted one to the other, what it is about this person that makes a lifetime together seem worth the effort. And it's forward to deeper understanding of what it means to say that God is love.

God as Father and Mother

Love is, by its very nature, life–giving. It first gives life to a couple themselves, creating a *we* out of the raw materials of *you* and *me*. A couple's love for one another spills over into relationships with in-laws and friends, coworkers and fellow parishioners. And, sooner or later, it seeks to take separate flesh in children.

In today's Catholic wedding ceremony, couples are asked to express their willingness to accept children from God. Would that were simple! On the one hand, it can be difficult to tailor child-bearing to one's physical, emotional, and financial resources. On the other hand, it is just plain painful to face the monthly news that no baby is on the way. (What happened to "I am fearfully, wonderfully made"?) Some couples will never bear or adopt a child. But with parents (and singles and vowed celibates), they are called to nurture life in their extended families, in their parish, and in the larger world.

Most couples will become parents and will discover that a child upsets the balance of a marriage long before proud new parents meet their offspring. Pregnancy brings morning sickness and hormonal storms; adoption is a harrowing process. And the little stranger whom two people cradle at last has evidently paid no attention to the details of their expectations!

Parents understand what it means to speak of God as loving Father or as the Mother who can never forget her child (see Isaiah 49:15). Giving birth is a brush against God, an awe-inspiring event.

Parenting teaches a new definition of love: not just gazing into each other's eyes, but looking outward together in the same direction. Children enlarge a couple's world. They bring other people into their lives: little playmates and their parents, teachers, best friends, first loves and future in-laws. And in their vulnerability new parents discover a sharper edge; they realize that what threatens any of the world's children—drugs, hunger, war— threatens their own. From PTA to Bread for the World, parents hear a call to shape the world their children will inherit.

Raising children takes its toll on a marriage. Sleepless nights with a newborn, endless trips to the soccer field and the library with older kids, the constant coming and going of adolescents, and the never-ending pressure to make ends meet leave little time, energy, or privacy for candlelight and romance, much less for serious conversation or unhurried lovemaking. Small wonder that couples rich in the grace of letting go begin to look forward to an empty nest, seeing it as a promising spot for another honeymoon!

The empty nest proves a quiet haven for these old friends. They can carry on a conversation without interruption, romp uninhibitedly, and fall asleep without listening for the door to close on the last homecoming teen. The struggle to establish a career winds down and, for many, a period of relative financial ease begins. Armed with a much surer sense of who they are than they had as newlyweds, they can focus on appreciating the different gifts they bring to their marriage.

Grandchildren give a new sense of one's place in history, and with it a need to explore traditions. Surely it is no coincidence that many people develop an interest in tracing the family history at this point. Grandparents have a faith-story to share with the newest generation.

Marriage in a New Setting

Retirement thrusts a couple back into the hard tasks of a new marriage. Living together full-time is not the same as sharing evenings and weekends and going separate ways during the day. Roles and responsibilities undergo redefinition, perhaps even a complete reshuffle of the arrangements that have worked for years. Finding new outlets for the energy once absorbed by a job, giving each other space to pursue separate interests: these draw in a new way on all the graces of marriage as a couple settles into their last years together.

In the beginning a man and a woman promised to love one

another "until death do us part." In the evening of life that parting is no longer just a possibility; it is inevitable. "Love is strong as death," the Old Testament poet wrote (see Song of Solomon 8:6). Of the three things that last (faith, hope, and love) love is the greatest (see 1 Corinthians 13:13). The conviction that those words are true carries a couple through years filled with both joy and sorrow. Sometimes they disappoint each other; often they start over again. Throughout a sacramental marriage, God stays always near, always calling a couple ever closer to each other in love.

As one of the prayers in the marriage rite proclaims, love is our origin, our constant calling and our fulfillment in heaven. As a believing community, we have a stake in every Christian marriage. The spirituality of married people enriches the life of the whole parish. They model for us the many ways of living out our vocations, whether we are married or not. Love, after all, is our common calling as Christians, whatever our state in life.

The Catholic Church solemnly teaches that:

> Married love is an eminently human love because it is an affection between two persons rooted in the will and it embraces the good of the whole person; it can enrich the sentiments of the spirit and their physical expression with a unique dignity and ennoble them as special elements and signs of the friendship proper to marriage.

The Lord, wishing to bestow special gifts of grace on it, has restored, perfected and elevated it. A love like that, bringing together the human and the divine, leads the partners to a free and mutual giving of self, experienced in tenderness and action, and permeates their whole lives. (*Gaudium et Spes,* 49)

Questions for Reflection

1. Why do we call marriage a sacrament?
2. Whose marriages have been inspiring signs for you? How?
3. In what way do marriages affect society at large?

CHAPTER TWO

Why the Sacrament of Marriage Makes a Difference

The Catholic Church teaches that "marriage and married love are by their nature ordered to the procreation and education of children. Indeed children are the supreme gift of marriage and greatly contribute to the good of the parents themselves.... But marriage is not merely for the procreation of children.... Even in cases where despite the intense desire of the spouses there are no children, marriage retains its character of being a whole manner and communion of life..." (*Gaudium et Spes*, 50).

In this chapter Janet Duccilli Daniel and Mitch Finley discuss not only why people marry, but also why the sacramentality of marriage is important for the couple, for their family, and for the community around them.

Why Think of Marriage as a Sacrament?

Couples who experience marriage as a sacrament have a decided advantage over those who don't. When a husband and wife think of their marriage as a sign of God's love, they tend to make room for God in their marriage. They are open to God's help, they pray, they see their relationship as holy, they are prompted to forgive, to say "I'm sorry," to respect their spouses. They put their marriage and family in the context of God's plan. A couple in a sacramental marriage are not exempt from problems, but they have an added source of patience, wisdom, and love on which to draw.

The Catholic rite for marriage joyfully acknowledges,

> My dear friends, you have come together in this church so that the Lord may seal and strengthen your love in the presence of the Church's minister and this community. Christ abundantly blesses this love. He has already consecrated you in baptism and now he enriches and strengthens you by a special sacrament so that you may assume the duties of marriage in mutual and lasting fidelity.

Before they exchange their vows, the couple is thus reminded of the advantages of the sacramentality of their marriage.

Why Marry?

Janet Ducilli Daniel compiled a short list of some of the most common problems, expectations and needs which surface in married life. She suggested that before marrying couples should ask themselves and each other why they want to get married. There's probably no one right answer to this question, but there are a lot of wrong ones: to escape a bad situation at home, for example, or for financial security or because no one else is likely to ask. Even pregnancy ("having to get married") is hardly a sufficient reason for marriage especially if the couple is very young or their relationship isn't strong.

Attitudes toward marriage are important, too, especially in light of society's confused notions about what a marriage should be. Is it a permanent commitment, or something that can be easily gotten out of if things "just don't work out" or if one of the partners "just doesn't want to be married anymore"? Is it a partnership, a dictatorship? Does one partner expect to be taken care of by the other? And what about fidelity? What values will marriage ensure?

Who's Going to Do the Dishes?

Decades ago, being a wife meant cooking, cleaning, and taking care of house and children. Being a husband meant being the breadwinner, disciplinarian, and decision-maker. Today that's not always the case. Husbands and wives are reexamining and redefining their roles.

Some couples, for example, take turns with cooking and cleaning chores. Whoever cooks doesn't have to clean up the kitchen afterward; she irons his shirts in return for a weekly car wash;

tasks like bed-making and laundry are done in turns. Some wives work while their husbands remain at home. Some couples even draw up contracts that specify who is responsible for which chore.

In practice, who does what is irrelevant as long as both partners are satisfied. So it's a good idea for engaged couples to discuss such issues as whether they will both hold outside jobs and how household tasks will be divided. They should also decide whether one partner will be responsible for decisions about financial matters such as investments or insurance or buying a new car, or whether those will be joint decisions.

Dependency vs. Independency

Some couples take the phrase, "And the two shall become one," literally. They go everywhere and do everything together. They remain glued to each other's sides at parties. Friends and hobbies they enjoyed separately before they were married are abandoned in favor of activities they can pursue as a couple. And the very idea that one might enjoy an evening away from the other's company is met with jealousy and hurt feelings: "You'd rather see a movie with Carol/go bowling with Richard than be with me!"

Other couples, on the other hand, act like married singles. Their paths cross occasionally at meals and bedtime and they sometimes go several days without even seeing each other. They share a name and a house, but not their lives.

Somewhere between these two extremes is a happy medium—an arrangement which gives the couple plenty of quality time together, yet allows for freedom to pursue individual interests. But that point is different for every couple. Couples need to be honest with each other about how much time they'd like to spend together and about things they'd like to do alone.

Couples also need to discuss how much freedom each will have with the opposite sex. If she has been having weekly lunches with a male friend, will he be upset by it? Will it bother her if he spends an entire evening at a party talking with a very attractive woman? Does "going out with the girls or guys" mean freedom to talk and dance with other men or women in bars or at parties? Jealousy is a destructive force in any relationship, but it's bound to occur if a couple hasn't agreed upon limits for acceptable behavior.

Extended Family Influences

Our families have a lot to do with our own expectations for marriage and family life. If her parents supplied all of her tuition and spending money through college, for example, she may find his refusal to do the same for their children disturbing. If his father never kissed his mother or showed affection for her in front of him, he may be uncomfortable with his wife's demands for affection.

Some couples have had the opportunity to observe each other's families at close range. She knows that his father is a strict disciplinarian, that his mother is gentle and understanding, and that they encouraged their children to excel in sports. He knows that her family placed great emphasis on doing well in school and choosing a career, that dialogue was used more than punishment in handling infractions, and that the family took interesting and often expensive vacations every year.

Sharing these things can bring partners closer together and give them insight into one another's behavior. It can also help them pinpoint things they liked about their family life, and what they'd like to change in their own family.

It's also a good idea for couples to draw up some ground rules to follow with their families. They should decide whether family members will be free to drop in at any time or are to wait for an invitation, and specify times at which they do not wish to be disturbed. An equitable arrangement for visiting and spending holidays with each family should also be determined.

Communicate, Communicate, Communicate

The open and honest communication and sharing of feelings that are so essential to building an intimate relationship requires effort and perseverance. Revealing one's inmost self to another person is scary because it carries the possibility of rejection. But the alternative is a lifetime of conversations that go no further than, "How was your day?" or, "What are we having for dinner?" That two people can spend their entire lives together and never really know each other is much more frightening. Knowing—and being known—intimately is worth the risk involved.

Consequently couples should take a careful look at the quality of their communication. Do they enjoy talking with one another? Can they share thoughts and feelings honestly without fear of ridicule or rejection? Does one partner try to manipulate the other through threats, tears, or sulking? Do they know how to handle conflict and express anger in constructive ways?

Money, Money, Money

Money is a major arena of marital conflicts. "Before we were married," a friend confessed recently, "Bob and I were sure we'd have no trouble living on the money we make. It seemed like so much at the time—we didn't even bother to draw up a budget." But, she admits, "I guess we weren't very realistic about how much things cost. Now we're in debt, our rent is going up, and I don't know where we'll come up with the money."

How much money does it take to live? Prior to marrying many engaged couples have no idea. They have lived at home all or most of their lives and have little experience with rent, insurance, grocery, utility, or doctor bills. And sometimes even those who have supported themselves for several years have trouble adjusting their spending habits to cover two people's expenses.

The best way to get an accurate picture of a couple's financial status is to draw up a budget. Before they can do that, however, they have to find out, in realistic figures, what they can expect to pay for housing, food, clothing, utilities, insurance, medical care, and so on. Then they can determine whether they'll have enough money to cover their expenses, and discuss whether adjustments will have to be made.

But that's not the end of the money discussion. Who is going to handle the money? Who will be responsible for seeing that bills are paid on time? Will savings and checking accounts be joint or separate? Will the couple have credit cards? How much can one spouse spend on a purchase without consulting the other? Will vacations, weekly movies, and dinner out be considered a necessity or a luxury? What are the couple's financial goals (a house in five years, a new car, a trip to Europe)?

Sex

Bob, who has been married eight years, smilingly recalls his anticipation of his wedding night. "I was sure I was going to make love to Judy eleven or twelve times," he says. "I had it all planned. After each time I was going to put a mark on the wall above the bed—a real testimonial to my virility."

But the next morning, he admits, there wasn't a single mark on the wall. "We were so exhausted after the wedding and reception, sleep was the only thing on our minds," Bob recalls. "But I ended up being glad we waited. There was much less tension when we were both rested and relaxed."

Bob and Judy's experience isn't unusual. Many couples discover their wedding night is not romantic and passionate, but simply the tiredest night of their lives—not exactly the optimum atmosphere for beginning a sexual relationship. To avoid feelings of failure and disappointment, engaged couples should be prepared for the possibility that nothing will happen—and remember to keep a sense of humor about what ever occurs.

And the same advice applies to couples long after their wedding night. Couples ought to discuss how often each one expects to have sexual intercourse. Are there sexual practices either feels to be immoral or embarrassing? Does the couple find each other attractive and expect to be comfortable with each other without clothes? Will they feel free to discuss their likes and dislikes, offer constructive suggestions, try new things? Do both feel comfortable with the idea of initiating sex?

Even those who have had premarital sex can benefit from a discussion of that relationship. Are they comfortable and satisfied with each other? How will their relationship change as they live out their marriage?

Children

How many children does the couple want to have? If she wants two and he wants ten, can they compromise? How will one partner feel if the other, for serious emotional or physical reasons, decides he or she would rather not have children at all? Would the couple consider adoption if they are unable to have children? If a couple decides to delay parenthood, what method of family planning will they use? Both partners must be comfortable with it. And since natural family planning methods require some preparation, it's important to discuss this well in advance. How will the couple feel in the event of an unplanned pregnancy?

And having children is just the start. Who will care for them once they arrive? If both spouses are working, will one "retire" to stay home with the children, or would they prefer a babysitter or day-care center?

What kind of discipline will the couple use? If he comes from a home where even minor infractions were punished with severe beatings, and she was never spanked as a child, the time to arrive at a shared philosophy of discipline is not after little Johnny commits his first offense. Will the couple share, equally in the task of disciplining children, or is one spouse to be responsible?

Religious Practices in the Marriage

For Catholics marriage is a sacrament and part of their life of faith. Have the couple ever discussed religion, their image of God, their beliefs and their doubts, their feelings about prayer? What part does religion play in their lives?

Some couples have a wedding in the Church because their wedding is important to them. They intend to maintain active participation in the Church after the wedding. Others have a Church wedding just to please Mom and Dad.

Couples of different denominations need to decide the best way they can practice their individual faiths and still share a faith-life together. And what about children? The Catholic party to the marriage promises to do what he or she can to assure the children are brought up Catholic. Is this agreeable to the non–Catholic party? How can children be taught respect and appreciation for both parents' faiths?

A couple who has carefully discussed all these issues is probably well-prepared for marriage. Yet no list of questions is exhaustive. There will always be surprises in the ever-changing relationship called marriage. Couples need flexibility, willingness to grow and a sense of humor. These qualities, and an abundance of love, are the best preparation for marriage a couple can have.

Thinking of marriage as a sacrament, recognizing its religious dimensions, and nourishing the spiritual life of both husband and wife provide an effective setting for coping with the problems of married life and promoting the joy and security that marriage is meant to bring.

Family Life Is Holy (Warts and All)

We conclude our analysis of why the sacrament of marriage makes a difference by looking at family life from Mitch Finley's perspective. He remembers an occasion when he was asked to talk to a group of parishioners about family life:

The pastor introduced me, and I rose from my seat and turned to face the audience of some sixty men and women. "Family life," I said, "is holy." Instantly, from the middle of the room, a man called out, "Ha!" which, naturally, drew laughter from the entire group.

My critic was only being honest, of course, and most of us, if we are honest, would tend to agree with him. *Holy* is not the first word that pops to mind for most of us when we think of family life.

The word *holy* tends to have an unreal sound; it smacks of a spiritual and moral perfection associated with rosy-cheeked plaster saints or nature untouched by human hands. We can call a brilliant sunset or a majestic eagle perched atop a tall pine tree holy; but a little knot of people who live together and squabble over who's going to take out the trash or what to watch on television? Fat chance.

We tag Mother Teresa holy because she cared for people she found dying in the gutters of Calcutta. But to call the typical family holy sounds like a weird joke. After all, in our family, you may protest, there's a ten-year-old who last year hit his younger brother over the head with a baseball bat so hard he had to have six stitches; a younger brother whose sole ambition in life, at present, is to one day own an electric bass guitar; a girl who collects postage stamps and hangs posters of rock stars on her bedroom walls; a beleaguered husband and father who commutes forty-five minutes to and from work every weekday and whose idea of a truly good time is watching the Super Bowl on TV; and a tired wife and mother who doesn't care what the kitchen looks like as long as she can spend a half hour in her flower garden each summer morning before she leaves for work.

Taking an Expanded View of Family

Family, we must recall, is a bigger word than we sometimes allow for. We want to take a more complete view of family here. Single people often feel left out when the conversation turns to "family life," but this should not be so. Just about everybody participates in some form of family life, even never-married adults. Single people continue to belong to an extended family of some kind. Often they have married brothers and/or sisters. Often they are aunts or uncles, as well as adult children who continue to have a relationship with their parents. Frequently, single people also have a network of friends who, in some sense, are "family" for them. And the family life single people participate in can be just as chaotic and stressful as any other form of family life.

Single people struggle with how to relate to their married brothers and sisters and their nieces and nephews. They sometimes feel taken advantage of. "What does my sister think I am," a single woman remarked, "a built-in babysitter, just because I'm single? I have a life of my own!"

A single man in his late thirties anguishes over his relationship with his parents. "They seem to think that because I'm not married, I should spend all kinds of time with them. I want to be available and help out when they need me, but I don't want to spend every weekend there."

No matter what form of family life we belong to, we are tempted to ask with a dash of skepticism: "*This* is holy?"

What Does Holy *Mean?*

It all depends, of course, on what we mean by *holy*. When the Bible says *holy*, it means "separate" or "different." The word implies being healthy and whole in a world where there is much that is unhealthy and fragmented. The English phrase "hale and hearty" sums up in excellent fashion the effects of true holiness. To be holy is to rejoice in oneself and in the gift of life. That which is holy is charged with enthusiasm for life. Holiness includes concepts such as humor and laughter, compassion and understanding, and the capacity to forgive and be forgiven, to love and be loved. That's what holiness is about.

What makes family life sacred is not to attain some kind of pristine perfection, but the fact that to live with people as lovingly as you can is to live with God. Remember that bleary-eyed wonder you sit across the breakfast table from each morning? Well—surprise, surprise—that person could be your path to closeness with God and may be as close as you'll ever get to God, this side of the grave.

What makes a family holy is not to be totally free from conflict or to become a group of people who never hurt one another. Rather, holiness in families comes from learning to forgive and be reconciled and learning to face up to our problems and do something about them.

In family life, *holy* means striving to surrender to God's light within us at times when the darkness around us seems overwhelming. It means struggling day after day to bring creative order—if only a bit—to the chaos. When we work at cultivating forgiveness, reconciliation, and community, we embody God's holy will in the context of family life.

I know a family that had to cope with an unwed pregnancy, and I would not hesitate to call this family holy. I know a family that discovered that a teenage daughter was sexually active and taking birth control pills, and this is a holy family, too. Holy families struggle with alcoholism, and holy families include teenagers who get involved with drugs. Holy families include those dealing with young single adults no longer living with their parents who decide to "live with" a boyfriend or girlfriend "without benefit of marriage." There are endless holy families that are struggling in pain with the effects of a divorce.

"I feel really bad," Bill says. "Mary Ann was reading the riot act yesterday afternoon to Tommy, who's fourteen, and he was giving as much as he was getting. He started talking in a very disrespectful manner to his mother, and I blew a gasket and got involved.

I started yelling at him to stop talking to his mother that way, he turned his anger on me, I reached out with a paperback book I had in my hand and smacked him on the arm, and that really set him off. We're screaming at each other, and finally I chased him upstairs to his room. He's up there yelling and banging things around. Talk about feeling depressed about the kind of father I am."

Later, however, Tommy came back downstairs calm and collected. "Sorry," Bill said as he briefly massaged the back of Tommy's neck. "Yeah, I'm sorry, too," Tommy said with a sheepish smile. "What's for dinner?"

In a holy family, people are frequently unkind to one another, but they keep on trying to love. Preparing meals, helping a teenager learn to drive, listening to one another, changing diapers, cleaning the house, tolerating chaos, and walking up and down with a fussy baby—all of this is done on holy ground.

Five Ways to See Holiness in the Midst of Family Chaos

1. **Give yourselves a pat on the back each day.** You are doing much better at being a parent, being married, being a single member of your extended family than you give yourself credit for most of the time. Accent the positive. Resist the inclination to be down on yourself because you think you don't measure

up to some otherworldly or unrealistic ideal. If ordinary family life was good enough for the Son of God to spend most of his earthly life in, it's good enough for you.

2. **Make the most of family meal prayer.** Light a candle, not just on special days, but *every* day. Maybe a single line from a song: "Amazing grace, how sweet the sound…". In ordinary language, thank God for one another and for this macaroni and cheese we are all about to wolf down, and for this milk, some of which somebody will probably spill….

3. **Share the good news of another's good example with your family.** For example, when you hear about some person or family coping courageously, spread the word. There's a man who washes windows every day and cleans office buildings until late every night. Do you know what he's doing? No, not washing and cleaning. He's putting his children through college.

4. **Remember that never, ever are you alone.** God loves you and wants to help you more than you know. Be consciously open to God's loving presence in your family life and struggles. Remember Psalm 127: "Unless the Lord build the house, they labor in vain who built it." Unless the Lord builds up and nourishes your family, you labor in vain.

5. **Build up bonds of mutual support with other family and friends.** Get together with families who are at about the same place in their family history as yours is. Organize a monthly discussion and prayer gathering for parents or for groups of single adults, to discuss and pray about their extended family relationships.

Questions for Reflection

1. Why is marriage difficult?
2. Is marriage ever fun?
3. What can parents do to make their family and home truly Christian?

How to Make the Sacrament of Marriage Work

Marriage was created by God. It is part of his plan. We know from human experience and the divine revelation that human nature suffers from a tendency to sin. We can see within ourselves as well as in others the pride, greed, anger, lust, envy, gluttony, and laziness which lead us into doing evil. The brokenness of human nature raises its ugly head in every relationship, including marriage. To live a full and loving married life couples must practice self-discipline, patience, humility, and perseverance. The Church offers us guidance and encouragement in the effort to do what is right, love what is good, and walk humbly in God's presence. The first step in making a sacramental marriage work is making room for God in married life. Fr. Richard Sparks, C.S.P., a moral theologian, offers us an overview of the United States bishops' letter *Human Sexuality: A Catholic Perspective for Education and Lifelong Learning.*

The Purpose of the U.S. Bishops' Document on Sex

Many adult Catholics, especially those who grew up in the pre–Vatican II era, remember trudging to church for confession on Saturdays or with their parochial school class on the afternoon before First Friday. Our laundry lists of sins almost invariably ended with what we considered "the really bad ones"—sexual sins of thought, word, or deed. Often we didn't even mention the word "sex." All we needed to say was that we had "impure" thoughts or talked "dirty" and the arena of sexuality was presumed and understood.

Whether deservedly or not, the Church has often been seen as the culprit that warped our view of human sexuality, making us see all matters sexual as suspect or potentially evil, and leading some to judge sex-related failings as the most serious sins of all. The Catholic bishops of the United States went a long way toward correcting this overly negative image when they adopted the document, *Human Sexuality: A Catholic Perspective for Education and Lifelong Learning.*

The bishops' document was written primarily to assist parents and religious educators, providing them with sound Christian guidelines for sexuality education. This chapter outlines some of the findings of the document and how a more complete understanding of human sexuality contributes to healthy marriages.

Human Sexuality: A Precious Part of God's Plan

According to the book of Genesis, God created all human beings in the divine image, male and female they were created. And God saw this man and woman, the crown of the sixth day of creation, as indeed very good. So, too, the incarnation of Jesus Christ, God becoming fully human, "adds even greater dignity or divine approbation" to the incarnate goodness of our being embodied as sexual beings (*Human Sexuality,* 10). Thus, the mystery and meaning of being human—embodied, incarnate, and therefore sexual—is intimately bound up in the mystery and life of God as Creator, Redeemer and life-giving Spirit.

Just as God is a Trinity, a mystery of mutual love within Godself, so too are we, created in God's image, called to this same universal vocation, "to love" and "to be loved." And our sexuality seems to be a core dimension of our experience of relating to others, our desire to move out from isolation to encounter, the first step toward true love. As the bishops define it, "*sexuality* is a fundamental component of personality in and through which we, as male or female, experience our relatedness to self, others, the world and even God" (*Human Sexuality,* 9).

The bishops speak of human sexuality as a wonderful gift, to be treasured, respected, and nurtured. So too, they speak positively about sex, a narrower reality, which refers "*either* to the biological aspects of being male or female (i.e., a synonym for one's gender) or to the expressions of sexuality, which have physical, emotional, and spiritual dimensions, particularly genital actions resulting in sexual intercourse and/or orgasm" (*Human Sexuality*, 9).

Acknowledging the potential for abuse or misuse of our sexuality—sometimes intentional (that is, sinful), often not—the bishops highlight the challenge, the "awesome responsibility" that befalls the steward entrusted with any precious gift.

Whether one is married, single or a vowed celibate, whether one is heterosexual or homosexual, and regardless of one's age or maturity, dealing creatively with sexuality remains a fundamental and lifelong task. The art of loving wisely and well is multifaceted. In First Corinthians, Paul reminds us that true love is "patient and kind, not self-seeking." Laying down one's life for the beloved is Jesus' benchmark for love at its fullest.

Chastity is a positive force for good and *the essential virtue needed to live one's sexuality responsibly and appropriately*, given each person's unique state in life. Often misunderstood as a synonym for the suppression or repression of sexual feelings, chastity "truly consists in the long-term integration of one's thoughts, feelings and actions in a way that values, esteems and respects the dignity of oneself and others" (*Human Sexuality,* 19).

God's Spirit abides and abounds. The grace to help us live sexually whole and chaste lives is readily available in so many ways—in ourselves, our families, the Church, the Word of God, the sacraments, prayer, the lives and witness of Mary and the saints, and "in the recesses of each human heart, where prayer, conscience formation and discernment find holy ground" (*Human Sexuality*, 21).

The Divine Plan Inscribed in Sexual Love

In chapter three the bishops cull from the Catholic tradition, and particularly the writings of John Paul II, in speaking about the "language" or "nuptial meaning" of the body. The Church teaches that human sexual intercourse is an action inscribed by the Creator with a twofold meaning, that is, with both a unitive and procreative dimension.

The Unitive Dimension

Lovemaking is an expression of vulnerability and intimacy, a two-in-one-flesh encounter, demanding a deep level of commitment and love for its natural fulfillment. Traditionally, this has been called the "unitive" meaning of sexual intercourse and, by extension, of marriage itself.

The Church finds affirmation for this unitive meaning of love, marriage and sex in the Genesis story of Adam and Eve—"It is not good for the man to be alone" (Genesis 2:18). The desire not to be alone, to love and to be loved—physically, psychologically, and spiritually—is a deeply rooted yearning. Drawing on Adam and Eve as a model, the Judeo-Christian tradition upholds marriage, called a "community of life and love," as the natural, God-given context for living together and lovemaking.

The Procreative Dimension

At the same time, if a man and women engage in sexual intercourse, the proximity of sperm and ovum can and, in the right circumstances, does produce new human life. Built into the very biology of genital sex is a "procreative" meaning. The story of creation, as recounted in Genesis chapter one, affirms that marriage and sexual union are also given for the procreation (and subsequent nurture and education) of children as well—"Be fertile and multiply" (Genesis 1:28).

Thus, the bishops echo the Scriptures, Church tradition, and their interpretation of what God intended in nature by concluding that marital commitment and fidelity provide the only stable environment in which genital sexual expressions find their true meaning as acts of loving union potentially open to procreation. "Prior to or separated from the marital commitment, sexual intercourse ceases to be an expression of *total* self-giving" (*Human Sexuality,* 33). The bishops conclude that "outside of this 'definitive community of life' called marriage, however personally gratifying or well intended, genital sexual intimacy is objectively morally wrong" (*Human Sexuality,* 33).

The Unitive/Procreative Formula

The bishops now apply both their more holistic view of sexuality and this twofold *unitive* and *procreative* formula to married partners.

Focusing on married couples, the document candidly discusses both marital commitment and responsible parenthood. Since love is not only or primarily about the present moment, couples getting married pledge themselves not only for the happy now, but also for the unseen future. Honesty, trust, open communication, hope, fidelity—sexual and otherwise—as well as faith in God, are the building blocks for lifetime commitments. "Each phase of marriage—the early years; the childbearing years or no-children years; mid-life crisis and the empty-nest years; senior years; and the inevitable death of one's covenant partner—has its own share of challenges" (*Human Sexuality*, 43).

The question of responsible parenthood is two-pronged: (1) questions related to spacing children and (2) the issue of reproductive technologies for couples having difficulty procreating. In both instances the *unitive* and *procreative* meanings come to the fore.

The Catholic tradition in recent decades has become more sensitive to the needs and desires of married couples to space responsibly the birth of children, both for the good of the couple and the well-being of the children conceived. As far back as 1951 Pope Pius XII taught that for "medical, eugenic, economic, and social" reasons a couple could reasonably avoid procreation "for a considerable period of time, even for the entire duration of the marriage" (*Address to Midwives*). At the same time, they may want and need to continue fostering their marital love through the unitive aspect of genital lovemaking.

It is the current teaching of the Catholic Church, however, that one ought to do such spacing "naturally," by making use of the biological ebb and flow of the woman's fertility cycle. "Since a woman is not fertile during the greater part of her menstrual cycle, a couple is respecting the natural 'rhythms' ordained by God if they 'make use of the infertile periods' for genital lovemaking, open to the possibility, however unlikely, of a child being conceived" (*Human Sexuality*, 46).

Regarding other birth control methods, the Catholic Church teaches that "a couple may never, by direct means (i.e., contraceptives), suppress the procreative possibility of sexual intercourse" (*Human Sexuality*, 47). It follows that direct sterilization surgeries are also prohibited, except in those instances when one is *directly* removing a diseased or cancerous reproductive organ, with the resultant sterilization being *indirect* and unintentional.

While the bishops hope that the logic of Natural Family Planning (that is, respecting one's natural rhythms) is compelling to married couples, they counsel pastoral sensitivity in dealing with "those who feel confused or who have genuine doubts about the wisdom of this teaching" (*Human Sexuality*, 47). As teachers the bishops must present the living tradition of the Church with clarity and conviction. As pastors, however, they strive to embody compassion and care "for all those who seek the truth with a sincere heart" (*Human Sexuality,* 48).

The bishops leave most questions related to reproductive technology to the fuller explanation of a 1987 document from the Congregation for the Doctrine of the Faith (a subsequent document, *The Dignity of the Person,* was issued by the Congregation for the Doctrine of the Faith in 2008 to help clarify and affirm what was said in the 1987 document and to address new questions). In summary fashion they note that just as it is inappropriate to engage in marital sex directly suppressing its procreative potential, so also procreation done "artificially"—artificial insemination, in vitro fertilization, surrogate motherhood and so on—breaches or inhibits the unitive or lovemaking dimension of sexual union.

Acknowledging that the desire for children is natural, the bishops express "deep compassion and empathy for those married couples who find themselves unable to conceive or bear children" (*Human Sexuality,* 48). They advocate adoption as one alternative, but note that professional counseling and ongoing pastoral care may be required to help childless couples deal with their own self-esteem, feelings, and sense of loss. With all due sensitivity, fertility is not guaranteed and what is "technically possible" (what one can do in terms of reproductive technology) is not identical with what is "morally admissible" (what one *may* or *ought to do*).

Overarching Concerns

Some sexual acts are diametrically opposed to the sacredness of human sexuality and undermine the integrity and beauty of married life:

Masturbation—"The Catholic tradition has consistently held that autoerotic or solitary genital sexual behavior is immoral and, in the objective sphere, can never be ethically justified" (*Human Sexuality,* 62). It breaches both halves of the procreative/unitive norm since it is neither procreative nor unitive in the interpersonal sense. However, in the realm of education and pastoral care, focus should be "on the development of the whole person, seeing these actions in context, seeking their underlying causes more than seeking to repress the actions in isolation" (*Human Sexuality,* 62).

Pornography—The bishops tactfully distinguish between art and pornography. Pornography is defined as "the use of visual or print media to present nudity and sexual activity in a degrading or depersonalizing way" (*Human Sexuality,* 63). It often preys upon society's most vulnerable members, making them into objects for the lustful and unloving sexual gratification of others.

Sexual abuse—Whether the instances of child abuse and sexual harassment and abuse are on the rise, or whether it is a matter of more candid reporting on these topics, these issues represent a personal and social tragedy in our midst. Victims, whether children or adults, need our compassion, our care, and our best medical, legal, and psychological assistance.

In Summary

The Catholic bishops of the United States have offered us a service in their document on human sexuality. While admitting that it is not the last word on the subject of human sexuality, they believe it is an important word.

"This document," they say, "is offered as our contribution to the ongoing discussion about what it means to be mature sexual persons—physically, psychologically, socially and spiritually whole.... We have presented a positive and hopeful Christian vision of what it means to be sexual and to be chaste" (*Human Sexuality*, 6, 83).

Questions for Reflection

1. What are the twofold dimensions of human sexual intercourse?
2. Why is pornography anti-marriage?
3. What advice would you give to a couple preparing to marry?

Conclusion

The Catholic Church cherishes marriage as "the one blessing that was not forfeited by original sin or washed away in the flood." In the nuptial blessing of the Marriage Rite, the Church prays:

> Father, you gave man the constant help of woman so that man and woman should no longer be two, but one flesh, and you teach us that what you have united may never be divided. You made the union of husband and wife so holy a mystery that it symbolizes the marriage of Christ and His Church. Keep this couple always true to your commandments. Keep them faithful in marriage and let them be living examples of Christian life. Give the strength which comes from the Gospel so that they may witnesses of Christ to others. And, after a happy old

age, grant them fullness of life with the saints in the kingdom of heaven.

Marriage can be difficult, but when it is embraced as a sacrament of salvation, when husband and wife allow Jesus to be with them and support their commitment, marriage becomes a source of grace and blessing for the couple, their families, their Church and the world.

Through this sacrament God unites man and woman in an unbreakable bond of love and peace. May the Father, Son, and Holy Spirit bless them in good times and in bad, in this life and in eternity. Amen.

When we started this analysis of marriage, it was suggested that by the time you got to this point you would be able to finish this sentence: "A sacramental marriage is…".

In the blank space below, jot down what you would say.

Sources

Most of the information in this book comes from:

Duccilli Daniel, Janet, "Ten Things You Should Discuss Before Marriage," *Catholic Update*, October, 1979.

Finley, Mitch, "Seeing Family Life as Holy, Warts and All," *Catholic Update,* October, 1992.

Luebering, Carol, "The Spirituality of Marriage," *Catholic Update*, May, 1997.

Richstatter, Thomas, O.F.M., "Sacrament of Marriage," *Catholic Update*, May, 1996.

Sparks, Richard, C.S.P., "Human Sexuality," *Catholic Update*, August, 1992.

Rite of Marriage, New York: Catholic Book, 1970.

Contributors

Janet Duccilli Daniel, is a freelance writer and former assistant editor for St Anthony Messenger Press.

Mitch Finley, is the author of over thirty books, and winner of eleven Catholic Press awards; he and his wife, Kathy, speak on issues related to marriage and family life; recent books include *It's Not The Same Without You: Coming Home to the Catholic Church.*

Carol Luebering, prolific author, one-time editor at St. Anthony Messenger Press; her books include: *Called to Marriage: Journeying Together Toward God* and *Open Your Hearts: Prayer Exercises for Engaged and Newly Married Couples.* Carol was married to Jack for fifty-four years; she died at the age of seventy-five in 2010.

Thomas Richstatter, O.F.M., has a doctorate in liturgy and sacramental theology from the Institut Catholique, Paris. He is currently teaching courses on the sacraments at St. Meinrad School of Theology, Indiana.

Richard Sparks, C.S.P., is a Paulist priest, pastor, teacher, moral theologian (his doctorate is from the Catholic University of America), popular speaker, and parish mission preacher.

Suggestions for Further Reading

Feister, John. "Seven Keys to Marriage," *Catholic Update,* July 2010.

Petitfils, Roy. *What I Wish Someone Had Told Me About the First Five Years of Marriage* (Cincinnati: St. Anthony Messenger Press, 2010).

Roberts, William. *Marriage: It's a God Thing* (Cincinnati: St. Anthony Messenger Press, 2007).

Vogt, Susan. *Parenting Your Adult Child: Keeping the Faith (and Your Sanity)* (Cincinnati: St. Anthony Messenger Press, 2010).

West, Christopher. *Good News About Sex & Marriage: Answers to Your Honest Questions About Catholic Teaching* (Cincinnati: Servant, 2004).

To order any of the above go online at
www.AmericanCatholic.org.

Your monthly publication
committed to adult faith formation from
St. Anthony Messenger Press

Call 1-800-488-0488 **for a FREE sample.**

- Explore Catholic tradition

- Understand the sacraments

- Explain Church teaching

- Encourage seasonal renewal

www.CatholicUpdate.com